THE ULTIMATE PLAYBOOK FOR REAL ESTATE FLIPPING

Mastering the Art of Real Estate Flipping for Maximum Returns

Katherine R. Walters

ISBN-13: 9798879131765
ISBN-10: 1477123456

Cover design by: Art Painter
Library of Congress Control Number: 2018675309
Printed in the United States of America

*This book is dedicated to those on the journey to a life well-lived
—individuals seeking vitality, purpose, and enduring well-being.
To every reader who opens these pages with curiosity and a thirst
for knowledge, may you find inspiration, practical wisdom, and
transformative insights.*

*To my loved ones, whose unwavering support has been the
cornerstone of my own journey, and to the countless individuals
whose stories have shaped the narrative of this book—your
resilience, courage, and pursuit of a meaningful life are the true
driving force behind these words.*

*May this book serve as a guide, a companion, and a source of
empowerment as you navigate the path to longevity, well-
being, and the fulfillment of your unique potential.*

THE **ULTIMATE PLAYBOOK** FOR **REAL ESTATE FLIPPING**

Mastering the Art of Real Estate Flipping for Maximum Returns

by

Katherine R. Walters

Table of Contents

INTRODUCTION

In "The Ultimate Playbook for Real Estate Flipping," you will find the definitive guide to navigating the ever-changing world of property investing and turning it into a viable business enterprise. This all-encompassing playbook is your guide to converting your ambitions of being a great real estate flipper into a reality. If you have ever fantasized about discovering the keys to that success, this playbook is your path.

Within the sphere of real estate, the art of flipping houses has arisen as a method of making smart investments as well as an entertaining and exciting experience. This playbook is not simply a collection of techniques; rather, it is an all-encompassing guide that is intended to provide you with the information, abilities, and insights that are necessary to master the delicate dance of property purchase, refurbishment, and resale.

Before we dig into the specifics of real estate flipping, let's take a moment to contemplate the fascination that pulls people to this ever-changing industry. Flipping houses isn't only about financial benefits; it's a journey packed with excitement, creativity, and the potential of converting neglected buildings into sought-after treasures. This playbook acknowledges the dual nature of real estate flipping, which involves striking a balance between the economic acumen necessary for lucrative investments and the passion and satisfaction that come with altering locations.

"The Ultimate Playbook for Real Estate Flipping" is not simply another how-to guide. The result of years of experience in the field, successful case studies, and a dedication to demystifying the complexity of real estate flipping are all included in this document. Whether you are an experienced investor who is trying to improve your tactics or a novice who is ready to enter the world of property transformation, this playbook is designed to meet you where you are in your journey.

The Things That You Should Anticipate

Comprehensive tactics: This playbook covers all parts of the real estate flipping process, from carefully selecting homes to performing efficient repairs and implementing effective resale tactics.

Actionable Insights: You won't find hazy notions here. Each chapter is packed with actionable insights, practical suggestions, and proven tactics that you can instantly implement to improve your real estate flipping ventures. These may be found scattered throughout the book.

Real-Life Case Studies: Beyond theories and techniques, we provide you with real-life case studies that highlight how individuals, just like yourself, have handled the hurdles and won in the field of real estate flipping.

A Holistic Approach: We know that successful real estate flipping is not only about money; it's about developing sustainable, pleasant businesses. This playbook includes a comprehensive strategy that addresses both financial advantages and the personal fulfillment that comes with property transformation.

As you begin on this adventure, consider it not only a guide but a partner. Whether you're flipping your first home or wanting to upgrade your existing techniques, this playbook is designed to empower you at every stage.

Get ready to learn the ultimate methods, grasp the complexities of property flipping, and design a road toward extraordinary success and joy in the domain of real estate.

PREFACE

Welcome to the preface to "The Ultimate Playbook for Real Estate Flipping." In these introductory pages, I express my warmest appreciation for choosing this playbook as your companion in the thrilling adventure of real estate flipping.

Real estate flipping is more than a business—it's an art, a science, and an experience. This intro acts as a handshake, an introduction to the concept that inspires this playbook, and a look into the transforming adventure we are about to embark upon together.

Before we dig into the methods and procedures, it's vital to understand what makes real estate flipping both an enticing endeavor and a practical investment. The essence rests not simply in the possibility for financial rewards but in the excitement of rejuvenating abandoned areas, turning them into homes that inspire and resound.

What distinguishes this playbook? Allow me to share: it's not just about flipping properties; it's about flipping the script on established tactics. This playbook amalgamates years of industry expertise, successful case studies, and a passion for encouraging individuals like you to prosper in the changing world of property transformation.

Our Commitment to You

- *Practical Wisdom:* Each page is loaded with practical wisdom, delivering ideas gained from the real-world experiences of successful flippers. This is not a theoretical handbook; it's a playbook built from the trenches of property flipping.

- ***Holistic Guidance:*** Beyond profitability, this playbook promotes a holistic viewpoint. It emphasizes that success is not just measured in monetary terms but also in the fulfilment received from constructing homes and communities.
- ***Adaptability:*** Whether you're a seasoned investor or a newbie, our techniques are meant to be adaptive. Consider this playbook a dynamic tool, developing with you as you negotiate the broad environment of real estate flipping.

As you turn the pages of this book, consider yourself not just as a reader but as an active participant in an exciting adventure. Your path will be defined by the tactics put forth here, but more importantly, by your unique insights, creativity, and commitment to mastering the art of real estate flipping.

In closing, consider this prelude as an invitation—an invitation to explore, learn, and start on a journey beyond the bounds of traditional real estate enterprises.

"The Ultimate Playbook for Real Estate Flipping" is more than a handbook; it's a spark for your success and fulfilment in the area of property transformation.

CHAPTER 1

Introduction to Real Estate Flipping

Welcome to the exciting universe of real estate flipping—a trip where abandoned houses become wealthy investments, and the art of transformation meets the science of profit. In this lengthy investigation, we will unravel the core of real estate flipping, following its historical growth, appreciating its allure, and realizing the hazards that accompany this dynamic business. This thorough chapter seeks to offer you a firm foundation, arming you with the information and insights required for navigating the convoluted world of property flipping.

Definition and Concept of Real Estate Flipping

At its heart, real estate flipping is a strategic investment strategy comprising the acquisition, rehabilitation, and eventual selling of properties with the primary purpose of producing a profit. This multilayered process involves a good awareness of market fundamentals, a discerning eye for property potential, and the ability to traverse the intricate landscape of real estate transactions. Flipping is not only a transaction; it is a transformational process that converts ignored homes into sought-after assets.

The Acquisition Phase

Flipping begins with the identification and acquisition of assets with unrealized potential. This step entails detailed market research, a review of property prices, and the discovery of prospects that correspond with your investment goals. The effective flipper must discriminate between discounted jewels and homes with potential dangers, creating the framework for a lucrative business.

The Renovation Phase

Once a home is bought, the rehabilitation process commences— a delicate ballet of creativity, finances, and project management. Renovations are not simply about aesthetics; they are strategic expenditures aimed at boosting the property's value. This section will look into budget-friendly remodeling ideas, high-impact renovations, and the art of combining cost and quality.

The Resale Phase

The climax of the flipping process is resale, where the altered property is positioned to attract purchasers promptly and at a premium. This entails smart marketing, recognizing market timing, and applying bargaining strategies to optimize results. The route from purchase to resale is a dynamic process that involves agility and strategic thinking.

Historical Overview and Evolution

To appreciate the core of real estate flipping, we must embark on a historical trip that spans decades of economic upheavals and housing market dynamics. The evolution of flipping reflects shifting cultural tendencies, economic cycles, and the altering nature of real estate as an investment. By knowing the historical backdrop, we acquire significant insights into the patterns, trends, and lessons that influence the landscape of property flipping today.

Early Ventures and Opportunistic Flipping

The roots of real estate flipping may be traced back to opportunistic operations where individuals spotted undervalued properties and changed them for a quick profit. Early flippers seized on market inefficiencies and shifting neighborhood dynamics to create value in the property market.

The Rise of Systematic Flipping

Over time, flipping moved from opportunistic initiatives to systematic, purposeful investments. The rise of real estate as a codified investment class and the proliferation of home remodeling television shows contributed to a more systematic approach to flipping. Investors began utilizing data-driven tactics and extensive market analysis.

Flipping in Contemporary Times

In current times, real estate flipping has become a lively and competitive profession. Technology, access to data, and a more sophisticated grasp of market patterns have converted flipping into a strategic investing technique. Flippers now traverse a complicated terrain, including technology, sustainable practices, and a comprehensive approach to property transformation.

The Appeal and Risks of Flipping Properties:

The draw of real estate flipping resides in its multiple appeal—the possibility for big gains, the gratification obtained from altering homes, and the dynamic character of the market. However, with enormous promise comes significant hazards, and prospective flippers need to recognize and minimize these problems.

The Appeal of Flipping:

Profit Potential: Real estate flipping has the potential for huge financial profits, making it an attractive investment option.

Creative Expression: Flipping allows individuals to exhibit creativity in altering houses, from design choices to unique restoration solutions.

Dynamic Ventures: The ever-changing nature of the real estate market lends an element of excitement and agility to flipping businesses.

Risks and Challenges:

Market Volatility: Flipping is impacted by market swings, and economic downturns can affect property valuations and resale possibilities.

Renovation Risks: Unexpected obstacles during renovations, from budget overruns to unanticipated structural issues, can pose risks to profitability.

Timing Challenges: The success of a flip is generally connected to market timing, and mistimed sales can impair returns.

The Dynamic Nature of Real Estate Flipping

Real estate flipping is neither a static nor one-size-fits-all undertaking. It demands agility, inventiveness, and an awareness of the ever-evolving dynamics of the real estate industry. This section sets the setting for the complex nature of flipping, emphasizing the necessity for a holistic approach that includes market trends, property circumstances, and the specific qualities of each enterprise.

Market Trends and Adaptability

- **Recognizing market fluctuations:** Successful flippers are alert to market trends, noting fluctuations in demand, price dynamics, and neighborhood developments.
- **Adaptability:** The ability to alter strategy based on market conditions is a crucial attribute of successful flippers.

Property-Specific Considerations

- **Property Conditions:** Understanding the state of a home, its potential, and the scale of improvements necessary are essential components in the flipping process.

- **Neighborhood Dynamics:** Factors such as neighborhood development, amenities, and local trends affect the attraction and resale potential of a property.

A Holistic Approach

- **Balancing Profit and Fulfillment:** Successful flippers know that wealth is not the main measure of success; personal pleasure earned from altering environments is also vital.
- **Sustainable activities:** A comprehensive approach integrates sustainable and eco-friendly activities, matching modern values and market trends.

Your Path Forward

As we complete this in-depth analysis of the introduction to real estate flipping, consider this chapter as the basis for the exciting chapters to follow. Whether you are a seasoned investor trying to develop your methods or a beginner ready to embark on the realm of property transformation, this playbook is geared to meet you where you are.

Your Aspirations

- **Crafting Your Vision:** Define your vision for real estate flipping, including your financial goals, artistic aspirations, and the effect you intend to create.
- **Investment Readiness:** Assess your preparation for real estate flipping, including criteria such as financial stability, risk tolerance, and market awareness.

The Journey Ahead

- **Navigating the Playbook:** Familiarize yourself with the layout of this playbook, which will take you through every stage of the real estate flipping process.
- **Embracing the Learning Curve:** Understand that real estate flipping is a constant learning process, and each venture contributes to your skills.

Cultivating the Flipping Mindset

- **Strategic Thinking:** Develop a strategic mentality, spotting possibilities, understanding risks, and devising adaptive tactics.
- **Passion for Transformation:** Cultivate a passion for transforming properties, seeing past the barriers to the possibilities for good change.

As we complete the introductory chapter, consider yourself on the brink of a transforming adventure. The world of real estate flipping beckons with potential for financial success, artistic expression, and personal fulfillment. The ensuing chapters will go further into the subtleties of each step, giving practical ideas, case studies, and expert viewpoints to assist you through the dynamic world of real estate flipping.

CHAPTER 2
Getting Started in Real Estate Flipping

Embarking on a path into real estate flipping takes a careful and strategic strategy. In this detailed chapter, we will dig into the basic stages for getting started, catering to both novices entering the realm of property transformation and seasoned investors wishing to develop their tactics. From assessing your preparation and defining clear goals to developing a knowledge foundation and constructing a realistic budget, this chapter acts as a compass, guiding you through the earliest phases of your real estate flipping business.

Assessing Your Readiness

Before plunging into the complexity of real estate flipping, it's necessary to undertake a self-assessment to measure your suitability for this dynamic business. Assessing your financial health, risk tolerance, and experience with the real estate market will set the tone for a successful flipping trip.

Financial Stability

Your financial foundation is a vital aspect in establishing your suitability for real estate flipping. Evaluate your present financial stability, evaluating aspects such as outstanding loans, credit score, and cash. A firm financial basis offers a cushion for any issues during property acquisition and improvements.

Risk Tolerance

Flipping inherently includes risk, from market volatility to unanticipated remodeling issues. Assess your risk tolerance, understanding that real estate markets may be unpredictable. Understanding and minimizing risks will be crucial to your success in the flipping world.

Market Awareness

A thorough grasp of the real estate market is vital. Research current market trends, property values in desired locations, and prospective prospects. Being alert to market trends will guide your property selection and overall flipping approach.

Setting Clear Goals and Objectives

Successful real estate flipping begins with a clear vision and well-defined goals. Establishing your objectives will drive your decisions throughout the flipping process, from property selection to resale techniques.

Financial Goals

Define your financial goals for each flipping attempt. Whether it's producing a specified profit margin, reaching a targeted return on investment (ROI), or developing a sustainable revenue stream, clarity on your financial objectives is vital.

Creative Aspirations

Consider the creative elements of property change. Define your aesthetic tastes, the desired amount of remodeling participation, and the overall mood you aim to create in the buildings you flip. Balancing financial aims with creative aspirations will form your distinctive approach to flipping.

Long-Term Vision

Look beyond individual flips and evaluate your long-term vision for real estate flipping. Are you looking for a portfolio of homes, growing a flipping company, or creating a legacy through judicious investments? Clarifying your long-term goal will guide the magnitude and breadth of your flipping attempts.

Building a Knowledge Foundation

In the evolving environment of real estate, information is your most significant asset. Building a firm foundation of information spans different dimensions, from market dynamics to property assessment procedures.

Market Research

Immerse yourself in market research to uncover trends, opportunities, and possible difficulties. Analyze historical data, assess current market circumstances, and examine developing trends. A well-informed approach to market dynamics will help in strategic property selection.

Property Valuation Methods

Understand the procedures used to assess property values. From comparable sales research to income capitalization methodologies, comprehend the subtleties of property valuation. This information is vital for finding undervalued assets with the potential for lucrative transformation.

Legal and Regulatory Considerations

Navigate the legal environment of real estate transactions.

Familiarize yourself with zoning restrictions, permit procedures, and other legal factors that may affect your flipping enterprises. Compliance with legal and regulatory norms is vital for effective operations.

Creating a Realistic Budget

A reasonable budget is the foundation of effective real estate flipping. It entails not just evaluating costs but also allocating resources strategically to optimize returns.

Projecting Acquisition Costs

Projecting the expenditures involved with property buying entails more than the purchase price—factor in closing costs, prospective financing fees, and any extra charges associated with property transfer.

Renovation Budgeting

Craft a precise remodeling budget that incorporates all areas of home improvement. From supplies and labor expenses to unanticipated obstacles, a detailed budget guarantees that your remodeling activities remain on track and within budgetary constraints.

Holding Costs and Contingencies

Account for holding costs, including property taxes, utilities, and mortgage payments over the holding term. Additionally, develop contingency savings to meet unanticipated needs. A strong budget anticipates unforeseen issues, minimizing the impact on your total profitability.

Leveraging Financing Options

Understanding and utilizing numerous funding alternatives is crucial to real estate flipping. While cash purchases give simplicity, financing helps you to expand your flipping operations wisely.

Traditional Lenders

Explore funding possibilities with traditional lenders, such as banks and mortgage organizations. Understand the regulations, interest rates, and conditions involved with traditional loans. Building a good financial profile boosts your eligibility for competitive lending arrangements.

Alternative Financing Methods

Consider alternate finance alternatives, including private lenders, hard money loans, or partnerships. Your option has its intricacies, and picking the correct funding technique for your enterprise may maximize your capital structure.

Calculating Financing Costs

Calculate the expenses connected with financing, including interest rates, loan origination fees, and potential prepayment penalties. A comprehensive study of finance expenses ensures that they line with your budget and contribute favorably to your total profitability.

CHAPTER 3

Flipping Houses for Fast Real Estate Profit

This works by purchasing houses in need of either modest cosmetic repairs or major renovations, performing the work, and then selling the home for a much higher price. In principle, this generates a considerable amount of wealth in a short length of time.

This is true for many people who try to flip houses, but it needs more than just a concept to make the process work. As a result, many people wind up sacrificing profit or losing money since their strategies aren't well thought out.

If you are thinking about getting into real estate investment, this is one of the easiest methods for investors to benefit. It is also a way to generate a large profit in a short period.

Unfortunately, this once-closely kept secret has gained some notoriety, and there is tremendous rivalry for the market's cheap assets as more investors decide to enter the collective ring.

If you're thinking about real estate investments in general and home flipping in particular, there are a few things to consider.

1) Treat this like a business, not a pastime. Far too many

investors need to take their investments seriously. This is a mistake since time is money in this market, and every month the home remains unsold costs you money. Make a plan and a timetable, and stick to it.

2) Remember that this is a business. You are not investing in properties to make friends or appear good. You are in business to make a profit. You cannot be afraid to make modest offers. The ability to purchase low and sell high is critical in this company.

This implies that you will almost certainly hurt people's feelings and anger them (since they frequently assign emotional values to their homes that are just not economically realistic). You must accept this truth to avoid achieving the huge earnings you desire. Nice men finish last, which is something you can't afford to do in this industry.

3) Pay attention to the marketplace. This is quite crucial. Many 'flippers' lost their shirts during the recent near-collapse of the housing market in the United States. The fact is that the indications have been mounting for many years. In cities where there was previously a scarcity of suitable housing alternatives, there are now surpluses.

This does not reduce the value of attributes; rather, it restores them to their appropriate values. Investors who expected to be able to sell for more than the property's true value were left holding the bag (or notes) on these properties for a long time before they could be sold.
Some were unable to sell their houses and were stuck with the additional price of the improvements.

Avoid buying in an inflated market, if possible, unless it is at the start of the inflation (before property developers have the opportunity to produce a surplus).

4) Don't let things become personal. Far too many first-

time house flippers choose to produce a piece of art over a commercial venture. When making cosmetic and structural renovations, it is tempting to go all out and build your ideal house.

The difficulty is that depending on the market, you are unlikely to repay the expenditures associated with doing so. The idea is to invest little and profit handsomely. Granite countertops are attractive, but they are unnecessary in a community populated by low-income residents. Instead of catering to your personal preferences, consider your target market's likes and expenditures.

Despite the hazards associated with flipping properties as a real estate investment, there is little doubt that fortunes have been gained doing so. Even in today's home market, there are a lot of opportunities for those who can complete the work swiftly and affordably. People still choose to acquire these magnificent residences rather than a property that requires renovations after the purchase price.

CHAPTER 4

Flipping Houses for Fun and Profit

Welcome to the center of real estate flipping, where the marriage of financial gain and artistic pleasure transforms property endeavors into a dynamic and entertaining undertaking. In this thorough discussion, we will dig into the strategic factors of flipping properties for both profit and personal joy. From integrating creativity into renovations to maximizing resale tactics for optimal financial returns, this chapter provides a thorough guide for anyone seeking not just monetary success but also a meaningful and joyful trip through the world of house flipping.

The Creative Dimension of Flipping

Real estate flipping transcends ordinary financial transactions; it is a canvas for creative expression. In this part, we'll discuss how integrating creativity into every stage of the flipping process may boost the attractiveness of properties and contribute to a fun and distinctive flipping experience.

Design and Aesthetics

Consider the aesthetic features of property change. From color palettes to architectural features, careful design decisions may boost the overall appeal of a house. We'll look into ideas for building rooms that are not only visually appealing but also resonate with potential purchasers.

Innovative Renovation Solutions

Embrace creativity in your refurbishment strategy. Explore imaginative solutions to common difficulties, from space efficiency to energy-efficient modifications. The inclusion of new concepts not only sets your flips distinct but also contributes to the property's long-term worth.

Personal Touch and Branding

Infuse your distinctive touch into the houses you flip. Consider building a distinctive brand identity for your enterprises, adding unique features that represent your personality. Building a renowned brand provides an added layer of value to your assets.

Crafting Profitable Renovation Strategies

Renovations are not only about beauty but also strategic expenditures aimed at enhancing property value. In this part, we'll study efficient remodeling plans that balance cost concerns to earn considerable financial returns.

Budget-Friendly Renovation Tactics

Explore budget-friendly restoration strategies that optimize expenses without sacrificing quality. From reusing existing features to smart enhancements, these strategies provide a cost-effective approach to property renovation.

High-Impact Improvements

Identify high-impact innovations that generate considerable returns on investment. We'll look into crucial areas such as kitchen and bathroom modifications, curb appeal additions, and technological integrations that greatly boost a property's market worth.

Efficient Project Management

Efficient project management is key for successful renovations. Explore ways for optimizing the remodeling process, including project scheduling, contractor collaboration, and efficient communication. A well-managed refurbishment assures prompt completion and minimizes potential delays.

Optimizing Resale Strategies

The ultimate aim of real estate flipping is a lucrative resale. In this part, we'll explore the subtleties of improving resale methods, from smart pricing to efficient marketing, to ensure a speedy and successful transaction.

Market Timing and Pricing

Understand the relevance of market timing in resale techniques. Explore ways for strategically pricing homes to attract possible purchasers while optimizing returns. We'll go into the art of pricing that balances market dynamics with property worth.

Effective Marketing Techniques

Marketing plays a crucial part in the reselling process. Explore successful marketing tactics, from professional staging to online listings and social media promotion. Crafting a captivating narrative around each property boosts its market appeal and speeds the sales process.

Negotiation Skills

Develop negotiation skills to manage the nuances of property deals. Whether working with buyers, sellers, or real estate brokers, efficient negotiating may impact the ultimate transaction price and terms. We'll review tactics for negotiating advantageous bargains that correspond with your financial objectives.

Navigating Challenges and Overcoming Setbacks

Real estate flipping is not without its obstacles. In this part, we'll cover frequent obstacles and problems experienced during the flipping process and suggest solutions for overcoming them.

Unforeseen Issues During Renovations

Explore techniques for managing unanticipated issues that may develop during restorations. From structural difficulties to unanticipated delays, contingency planning ensures that setbacks do not ruin your flipping efforts.

Market Fluctuations

Understand how to handle market volatility and economic risks. Strategies for responding to changing market conditions and making informed decisions in dynamic situations will be covered, promoting resilience in the face of external obstacles.

Balancing Profit and Personal Fulfillment

Achieving a balance between financial success and personal contentment is a fundamental aspect of real estate flipping. We'll discuss techniques for integrating your flipping activities with your own beliefs and ambitions, providing a more meaningful and rewarding experience.

Case Studies: Learning from Successful Flippers

Learning from real-life examples is crucial in the field of real estate flipping. In this part, we'll look into case studies of successful flippers, studying their techniques, obstacles, and achievements. These case studies give practical insights and motivation for your flipping initiatives.

Case Study 1: From Neglect to Luxury - A Transformative Renovation

Explore a case study where a neglected home receives a thorough renovation to become a magnificent residence. Learn about the remodeling plans, design decisions, and marketing approaches that led to the property's success in the market.

Case Study 2: Timing the Market – A Strategic Resale

Triumph

Delve into a case study that shows the relevance of market timing in the resale process. Analyze how planned pricing and excellent promotion lead to a rapid and lucrative resale in a competitive market.

Case Study 3: Balancing Profit and Passion – A

Fulfilling Flipping Journey

Explore a case study where a flipper effectively blends financial prosperity with personal fulfillment. Gain insights on how combining corporate aims with personal beliefs may lead to a more productive and joyful flipping experience.

CHAPTER 5
Benefits of Flipping Real Estate

This is one immensely tangible benefit, particularly when the profits are large and fast to come your way. Of course, there are hazards. Most ventures that offer high profits also come with a high degree of risk. Money, however, is not the only benefit that can be associated with reselling real estate, though it is undoubtedly the one on most investors' minds when they get into this line of work.

Let's talk about profit first. Profit is the one reason that most people get into this business. The days are lengthy, and the work is demanding. This is obviously different from the type of work one would customarily undertake for the simple joy of getting one's hands dirty.

This is actual labour that leaves you bone weary at the end of the day. However, when all the work is done, and you get around to making the transaction, you will find that the profit involved in a successful turn is well worth the effort you've put into the process.

The good news is that the astute investor can still manage to make money even when the situation may not work out quite as anticipated. This is yet another benefit to reselling real estate. If the transfer doesn't work out, there is always the option of leasing to own the property or renting the property out.

The profits in these situations are considerably less than a straight-out flip, but it can prevent financial disaster, which is often the risk of a flip gone awry. The fact that there are options and that you aren't necessarily left ruined at the end of a poor turn is undoubtedly a benefit. There are a few types of investments that enable you the option to save yourself the way real estate does.

One of the intangible benefits of converting properties is that you are, in essence, working for yourself. In other words, you do not have to press a time clock or fret about overtime (at least not on your part). This can be a negative thing, too, if you need more discipline to get the job done. However, most of us will view this as an enormous check in the pros column when considering whether or not to take the plunge into the amazing and terrifying world of real estate investing.

Even though this is a business that requires a lot of work in order to turn an attractive profit, there is some satisfaction at the end of the day involved in knowing that you are working for yourself and not to make someone else affluent or in order to strike a time clock.

That sensation of gratification is one that you should hold onto when the brand-new toilet you've just installed becomes a geyser. Of course, there are errors along the road; what other job keeps you on your toes quite like this one?

Real estate investing, house turning, in particular, can be one of the most exasperating types of investments a soul can pursue. At the same time, it can also be one of the most rewarding mentally, spiritually, and financially. This is something you should bear in mind when deciding whether or not this is the correct path for you.

CHAPTER 6
Sourcing and Acquiring Properties

In the intricate ballet of real estate flipping, success begins with acquiring the appropriate properties. This Chapter is a comprehensive investigation of the art and strategy behind sourcing properties and navigating the acquisition process. From identifying lucrative opportunities to negotiating deals and mitigating risks, this exhaustive guide will equip you with the knowledge and insights required to make informed decisions in the dynamic landscape of property acquisition.

Identifying Lucrative Opportunities

Sourcing profitable properties begins with an acute eye for potential. In this section, we'll examine strategies for identifying opportunities that align with your flipping objectives and offer the potential for substantial returns.

Market Research and Analysis

Effective market research is the foundation of identifying lucrative opportunities. Dive into strategies for analyzing market trends, understanding neighborhood dynamics, and identifying emerging opportunities. Uncover the data-driven approach to recognizing areas with growth potential.

Networking and Industry Connections

Build a network of industry connections to remain informed about potential opportunities. From real estate agents and fellow investors to local professionals, cultivating relationships within the real estate community enhances your access to off-market deals and valuable insights.

Targeting Distressed Properties

Distressed properties often conceal significant potential. Explore strategies for targeting and assessing distressed properties, including foreclosures, short sales, and properties in decay. Learn to see beyond the surface and identify the latent value in neglected residences.

Financing Strategies for Property Acquisition

Once a prospective property is identified, navigating the financing landscape becomes crucial. This section delves into various financing strategies, ensuring you have the tools to secure properties within your budget and financial capabilities.

Traditional Financing

Explore traditional financing options, including mortgages and bank loans. Understand the eligibility criteria, interest rates, and terms associated with traditional financing. Learn how to present a robust financial profile to secure favorable loan terms.

Creative Financing Solutions

Consider inventive financing solutions that go beyond traditional methods. From seller financing to lease options, these strategies provide flexibility in procuring properties, particularly in situations where conventional financing may be challenging.

Evaluating Return on Investment (ROI) for Financing Options

Assess the return on investment for each financing option. Understand the impact of interest rates, loan terms, and associated costs on the overall profitability of your flipping venture. Make informed decisions that align with your financial objectives.

Navigating Property Inspections and Due Diligence

Before concluding a property acquisition, comprehensive due diligence is essential. This section guides you through the process of property inspections, assessing potential risks, and conducting comprehensive due diligence to avoid unanticipated challenges.

Importance of Property Inspections

Understand the significance of property inspections in the acquisition process. Learn to identify red flags, assess structural integrity, and evaluate potential renovation challenges. A meticulous inspection procedure ensures that you make informed judgments about the property's condition.

Conducting Due Diligence

Go beyond inspections and delve into comprehensive due diligence. This includes researching property history, assessing legal and title aspects, and comprehending zoning regulations. Thorough due diligence minimizes the risk of encountering unforeseen issues post-acquisition.

Environmental Considerations

Explore environmental considerations that may impact property acquisition. From hazardous materials to local environmental regulations, understanding and mitigating environmental risks is crucial for both the property's value and your long-term liabilities.

Negotiating Property Deals

Negotiation skills are paramount in acquiring properties at favorable terms. This section provides practical strategies for negotiating agreements that align with your financial objectives and contribute to the overall success of your flipping ventures.

Building Rapport with Sellers

Establishing rapport with sellers is the foundation of successful negotiations. Explore techniques for effective communication, active listening, and building trust with property owners. A positive relationship sets the stage for mutually beneficial negotiations.

Understanding Seller Motivations

Understand the motivations for moving property vendors. Whether it's a rapid sale, financial distress, or a desire for a hassle-free transaction, identifying vendor motivations provides insights that can be leveraged during negotiations.

Win-Win Negotiation Strategies

Adopt win-win negotiation strategies that create value for both parties. From flexible closing dates to addressing seller concerns, negotiate terms that align with your objectives while respecting the requirements of the property seller.

Mitigating Risks in Property Acquisition

Real estate comes with inherent risks, and comprehending how to mitigate these risks is crucial. This section examines risk mitigation strategies to safeguard your investments and ensure a seamless acquisition process.

Title Insurance and Legal Protections

Explore the importance of title insurance and legal protections in property acquisition. Understand how these safeguards can protect you from unforeseen legal complications, disputes, or title issues that may arise during or after the acquisition.

Contingency Planning

Develop contingency plans to address potential challenges. From unexpected repair costs to changes in market conditions, having contingency plans in place ensures that your acquisition strategy remains adaptable and resilient.

Professional Advisors and Consultants

Engage professional advisors and consultants to navigate complex aspects of property acquisition. From real estate attorneys to property assessors, assembling a team of experts enhances your ability to identify and address potential hazards.

Case Studies: Successful Property Acquisitions

Delve into real-world case studies of successful property acquisitions. Analyze the strategies, negotiations, and risk mitigation techniques employed by experienced flippers to secure properties that contributed to their overall success.

Case Study 1: Strategic Acquisition in a Growing Neighborhood

Explore a case study where a speculator strategically acquires a property in a neighborhood experiencing growth. Understand the market analysis, negotiation strategies, and due diligence process that contributed to a successful acquisition in a burgeoning area.

Case Study 2: Navigating Legal Complexities for a Distressed Property

Analyze a case study where a speculator effectively navigates legal complexities to acquire a distressed property. Learn about the significance of legal due diligence, negotiation strategies with distressed property owners, and mitigating risks in challenging situations.

Case Study 3: Creative Financing for a Unique Property

Delve into a case study where inventive financing solutions are employed to acquire a distinctive property. Explore how non-traditional financing methods contribute to the successful acquisition of a property with distinctive characteristics.

Envision yourself endowed with the knowledge and strategies required to navigate the complex landscape of property acquisition. Identifying opportunities, procuring financing, conducting due diligence, negotiating agreements, and mitigating risks are integral components of the acquisition process.

Each property acquisition is a step closer to realizing your flipping goals and constructing a portfolio of profitable ventures in the dynamic world of real estate. In the intricate ballet of real estate flipping, success begins with acquiring the appropriate properties.

CHAPTER 7

Choosing Your Real Estate Appraiser

If you intend to finance your home through a bank or other loan, you'll more than likely need to get the property evaluated first. Banks and most lenders want to know the value of the home for your safety, as well as make sure that the home they are financing is worth the entire amount that you take on the loan.

In most cases, the assessment suggests that the residence does indeed meet or exceed the asking price. In some cases, however, the assessment will come back, saying that the residence is worth less than the sale price. If this is the case, the buyer usually has to either drop the transaction or attempt to negotiate with the seller to get a price that meets the evaluation.

For those very reasons, a real estate evaluator is very essential. When you are working with a property, one appraisal can make a transaction or break it. Even though you may not be financing your purchase through a lender or bank, you should still make an effort to get the home evaluated and find out its true value.

You should also make sure to discover the finest expert that you can pay. If you hire an appraiser who isn't that experienced, you'll pay for it later when you discover that the property isn't worth what you paid for it.

A real estate appraiser will go through the property, make an evaluation, and then provide you with a written assessment after he has compiled all the necessary information. Appraisers will also take into consideration the substitute costs as well. Also, they will have to alter land listings as well. There is a lot of work involved with appraisals, which is why it's so very essential that each stage of the process is handled properly by a qualified real estate appraiser.

If you have a real estate professional, they will more than likely be able to make a recommendation. Keep in mind that this doesn't indicate that
he/she is the finest; it's just someone who your agent works with. To ensure that you get the correct estimate on your home, you'll need to find yourself an appraiser who is capable of finishing the task.

When you search for your real estate inspector, you should look for someone who comes highly suggested. You can ask family and friends for their views or consult local publications, even the Internet. If you take your time and search for the finest real estate appraiser that you can find – you'll usually get an estimate that is right on target.

CHAPTER 8
Financing Your Flip

In the delicate world of real estate flipping, the capacity to get finance is a vital component that may define the success and profitability of your operations. Chapter 8 is a detailed analysis of the many funding possibilities available to flippers, giving in-depth insights into standard and innovative ways. From negotiating loans and mortgages to exploring unique financing methods, this chapter offers a roadmap to help you effectively fund your flips.

The Importance of Strategic Financing

Strategic finance is the cornerstone of a successful real estate flipping company. This section elucidates the relevance of matching your financial approach with your flipping goals, stressing the influence financing decisions may have on your total profitability.

Understanding the Financial Landscape

Navigate the financial environment of real estate flipping, including market movements, interest rates, and economic situations. Develop an awareness of how external circumstances might impact funding possibilities and shape your entire approach.

Tailoring Financing to Your Objectives

Recognize the range of flipping objectives and how they might impact your funding options. Whether you're focusing on rapid flips for short-term returns or creating a long-term portfolio, adjust your financing method to correspond with your individual goals.

Balancing Risk and Reward

Evaluate the risks and advantages associated with alternative funding choices. Striking a balance between risk and reward ensures that your financial selections contribute favorably to your bottom line while reducing possible setbacks.

Traditional Financing Options

Traditional funding techniques give stability and comfort. In this part, we dig into the typical routes of collecting financing for your flips, evaluating the advantages and downsides of each.

Mortgage Loans

Understand the mechanics of mortgage loans for real estate flipping. Explore the qualifying criteria, down payment requirements, and conditions connected with mortgages. Learn how to establish a good financial background to achieve favorable mortgage conditions.

Home Equity Loans and Lines of Credit

Leverage the equity in existing properties through home equity loans or lines of credit. Uncover the subtleties of tapping into your property's equity to fund new acquisitions or upgrades. Assess the risks and advantages of employing this funding approach.

Conventional Bank Loans

Explore traditional bank loans as a funding alternative. Understand the application procedure, interest rates, and payback periods related to bank loans. We'll explore tactics for creating a strong connection with banks to boost your loan acceptance prospects.

Alternative Financing Methods

Beyond established pathways, new finance alternatives provide freedom and innovation. This section dives into non-conventional techniques, giving insights into their usefulness and implications.

Hard Money Loans

Hard money loans are a popular alternative among flippers for their speedy approval and flexibility. Explore the characteristics of hard money loans, including interest rates, loan-to-value ratios, and the use of collateral. Learn when and how to utilize hard money funding efficiently.

Private Lenders and Investor Partnerships

Engage private lenders or develop collaborations with investors to get financing for your flips. Uncover the benefits and pitfalls of dealing with private lenders and investors. Learn how to build agreements that match both sides' interests.

Seller Financing

Seller financing offers a unique arrangement where the property seller acts as the lender. Understand the mechanics of seller financing, including negotiating methods and the parameters that can be negotiated. Evaluate whether seller financing is a suitable choice for your flips.

Creative Financing Solutions

Creativity in funding can offer doors to unusual opportunities. This section investigates unique finance options that go beyond typical ways, giving a toolset for novel funding alternatives.

Lease Options

Explore the notion of leasing options as an innovative financing alternative. Understand how leasing alternatives operate, the benefits they offer, and when to consider adding them to your financing plan. Evaluate cases when leasing alternatives correspond with your flipping aims.

Subject-To Financing

Subject-to-finance includes acquiring a property subject to the current mortgage. Delve into the complexity of subject-to-play deals, including due diligence, legal issues, and the possible advantages of this unorthodox financing approach.

Wraparound Mortgages

Understand the idea of wraparound mortgages and how they may be employed for real estate flipping. Explore the benefits and hazards connected with wraparound mortgages, along with instances when they may be a smart financing alternative.

Evaluating Financing Costs and ROI

Effective finance decisions demand a holistic grasp of costs and profits. This section helps you through the process of assessing financing costs and determining return on investment (ROI) to make educated choices.

Calculating Financing Costs

Understand the different expenses connected with borrowing, including interest rates, fees, and potential penalties. Learn how to assess the entire financing expenses for each funding type, enabling you to evaluate and make cost-effective selections.

Estimating Return on Investment (ROI)

Estimate the return on investment for your flips based on

different funding options. Consider the impact of financing expenses on your total profitability and analyze whether your financing strategy matches your ROI targets.

Risk Mitigation in Financing

Explore ways to minimize risks related to finance. From diversifying financial sources to developing contingency plans, good risk mitigation ensures that your businesses stay strong in the face of unanticipated crises.

Case Studies: Financing Success Stories

Learn from real-world examples with case studies of successful finance techniques. These case studies give practical insights into how skilled flippers strategically leveraged money to attain lucrative outcomes.

Case Study 1: Leveraging Hard Money for Quick Turnaround

Explore a case study where a flipper effectively uses hard money funding for a speedy turnaround. Understand the decision-making process, risk factors, and financial results connected with this financing option.

Case Study 2: Creative Financing for Unique Property

Delve into a case study where unusual finance strategies are applied for a unique property. Analyze how unorthodox financing strategies help to the successful acquisition and transformation of a property with unusual attributes.

Case Study 3: Private Lender Partnership for Portfolio Growth

Analyze a case study where a flipper creates a collaboration with a private lender to promote portfolio expansion. Explore the intricacies of this financing structure, the conditions agreed upon, and the overall influence on the flipper's long-term aspirations.

CHAPTER 9

Things to Avoid When Flipping Real Estate

The truth of the matter is that this is one of the more engaging methods for many investors who are simply 'itching' to get their hands a little soiled.

The labor equity involved in these transactions, while attractive, can also be daunting when skills are inadequate and out and out hazardous in some situations.

Suppose you are one of the many around the world who contemplate the allure of converting property with enormous dollar signs in your eyes. In that case, you should avoid the following things in order to minimize your risks while maximizing your potential for success.

1) Remember to have a qualified inspection of the property before any money changes hands. If you do not have any concept of the categories of work that need to be done, then you cannot make an educated estimate of the costs involved in rehabbing the property.

2) Remember to underestimate the budget for maintenance on the reverse. This is one of the most common errors that even seasoned professionals make, and it can mean the difference between a profit and a loss on the property if you aren't careful and do not adhere to the planned budget.

3) Do not exaggerate your abilities. This is another common error.

The fact that you've seen something done on television doesn't mean that it is something you can do on your own. It costs more money and time to have someone come in and repair your errors than to have a professional do the work from the outset.

You can still learn how to do some of the tasks or that doing so would be cost-effective. The trick resides in determining where your skills and abilities can really take you rather than where you expect they will take you. Plumbing, electrical, and structural work are generally best left to the professionals unless you have specific experience or training in these disciplines.

4) Remember to hold yourself accountable to your timetable and your budget. Real estate investing places you in the boss's seat, and while that is often simple when it comes to driving others, we often have difficulty holding ourselves accountable for time and money along the road. Unfortunately, neglecting to do so can be a very costly blunder.

5) Remember to keep up with invoices, bills, etc., and reconcile the facts and figures daily. It is far too simple to allow a couple of visits to the local home improvement center to avoid scrutiny.

Add a couple of these excursions per day, and you could easily discover thousands of dollars missing from your budget with no paper trail to explain the transactions. You could also discover that some tools will not function or be needed for the project. Those items can only typically be returned with the original invoices.

6) Avoid having too many executives in the endeavor. If this is your ball game, then you need to run with it rather than having 10 persons giving contradictory directives. Schedule meetings routinely to discuss progress and any adjustments or changes that may need to be made.

7) Avoid inadequate planning. This is one phase that is the difference between success and failure for many would-be house exchangers. Plan out every step of the undertaking in an order

that makes logic. You do not want to paint the ceilings or walls after you've installed new floors. Do you want to tear out walls in order to replace infrastructure after you've painted them?

Plan things out in the proper order and allow a day or two between subsequent endeavors in case extra time is required. The last thing you want to do is pay a group of contractors to stand around waiting for the paint to cure so they can begin the next phase in the process.

There are hazards involved in any form of investment. While real estate is one of the finest things in the world in which people can invest, there are still dangers involved.

Following the advice above, however, can substantially lower those risks and give investors the opportunity to have great expectations when all is said and done. Whether this will be your first flip or your fortieth flip, there is much that can be reviewed in the steps above that will reaffirm many of the things you've learned along the way.

CHAPTER 10
Planning and Executing Renovations

Renovations are the transforming heartbeat of real estate flipping, influencing the potential and value of a home. Chapter 10 digs into the difficult process of planning and executing renovations, leading flippers through the processes of changing a house into a desirable and lucrative asset. From strategic planning to hands-on implementation, this chapter presents a complete path for optimizing the impact of renovations on your real estate flipping endeavors.

Strategic Renovation Planning

Crafting a Vision for the Property

A typical error in real estate flipping is commencing on improvements without a clear vision for the property. Flippers who lack a well-defined vision may need help in selecting coherent design decisions, thereby decreasing the property's overall attractiveness.

Solution: Develop a Comprehensive Vision

Prioritize the creation of a holistic vision for each site. Consider the target market, neighborhood aesthetics, and current design trends. This concept will act as the guiding principle for renovations, delivering a unified and appealing result.

Budgeting for Renovations

Underestimating Renovation Costs

Only overestimating remodeling expenses is a key error that may stretch budgets and damage profitability. Flippers who need to appraise the entire extent of renovations adequately may find themselves with financial issues mid-project.

Solution: Detailed Budgeting and Contingency Planning

Create a precise remodeling budget that incorporates all components of the project, including materials, labor, permits, and probable contingencies—factor in a contingency reserve to accommodate for unanticipated obstacles. A rigorous planning technique guarantees financial flexibility and avoids the possibility of budget overruns.

Identifying Key Areas for Improvement

Overlooking High-Impact Areas

Neglecting to identify high-impact areas for improvement might result in unsatisfactory upgrades. Flippers who neglect critical areas may lose opportunities to boost the property's value and charm.

Solution: Prioritize High-Impact Upgrades

Conduct a thorough assessment of the property to identify high-impact areas for improvement. Focus on key spaces such as kitchens, bathrooms, and curb appeal. Prioritize upgrades that resonate with potential buyers and contribute significantly to the property's overall value.

Crafting a Renovation Timeline

Setting Unrealistic Timelines

Setting unrealistic renovation timelines is a common pitfall that can lead to rushed decisions and compromised quality. Flippers who need to pay more attention to the time required for renovations may find themselves facing delays and challenges.

Solution: Realistic Project Planning

Develop a realistic renovation timeline based on the scope of work, local regulations, and potential challenges.

Factor in contingencies for unexpected delays, ensuring that the renovation process remains on schedule without sacrificing quality.

Selecting Quality Materials and Finishes

Opting for Subpar Materials

Choosing subpar materials can negatively impact the quality and longevity of renovations. Flippers who prioritize cost over quality may compromise the overall appeal and marketability of the property.

Solution: Invest in Quality Materials

Prioritize quality when selecting materials and finishes for renovations. Opt for durable and aesthetically pleasing options that align with the property's target market. Investing in quality materials enhances the property's value and ensures long-term satisfaction for buyers.

Sustainable and Energy-Efficient Upgrades

Overlooking Sustainable Practices

Neglecting sustainable and energy-efficient upgrades is a missed opportunity for flippers. Buyers increasingly value eco-friendly features, and overlooking these upgrades may result in a property that needs more modern appeal.

Solution: Integrate Sustainable Practices

Explore sustainable and energy-efficient upgrades as part of your renovation strategy. Consider options such as energy-efficient appliances, smart home technology, and eco-friendly materials. Integrating sustainable practices not only attracts environmentally conscious buyers but also enhances the property's marketability.

Managing Renovation Contractors

Poor Contractor Selection

Choosing inexperienced or unreliable contractors can lead to delays, cost overruns, and subpar artistry. Flippers who need to vet and manage contractors effectively may encounter challenges during the renovation process.

Solution: Thorough Contractor Evaluation

Thoroughly evaluate and select contractors based on their experience, reputation, and past work. Obtain multiple quotes, check references, and ensure clear communication throughout the project. Effective contractor management is essential for successful renovations.

DIY vs. Professional Services

Overestimating DIY Abilities

Overestimating one's DIY abilities can lead to substandard work and additional costs. Flippers who take on tasks beyond their expertise may compromise the quality of renovations and impact the property's overall appeal.

Solution: Assess DIY Capabilities Realistically

Assess your DIY capabilities realistically and delegate tasks that require professional expertise.

While DIY projects can save costs, prioritizing quality artistry ensures that renovations contribute positively to the property's value.

Staging for Maximum Impact

Neglecting Property Staging

Neglecting property staging is a missed opportunity to showcase the property's potential. Flippers who overlook staging may present a property in a less appealing light, potentially affecting its marketability.

Solution: Prioritize Professional Staging

Prioritize professional staging to enhance the property's visual appeal and help potential buyers envision the space. Work with experienced stagers who understand the target market and can highlight the property's key features. Effective staging contributes to a quicker and more lucrative resale.

Navigating Unexpected Challenges

Failure to Anticipate Challenges

Renovations often come with unexpected challenges, and flippers who fail to anticipate and address these challenges may find themselves overwhelmed and stressed during the process.

Solution: Develop Contingency Plans

Develop comprehensive contingency plans to address potential challenges that may arise during renovations.

Whether it's unforeseen structural issues, delays in material deliveries, or weather-related setbacks, having contingency plans in place ensures a more resilient and adaptable renovation process.

Case Studies: Successful Renovation Stories

Explore real-world case studies of successful renovation strategies. Analyze the decisions, challenges, and outcomes of experienced flippers who executed renovations that significantly contributed to the success of their real estate flipping ventures.

Case Study 1: Transformative Kitchen and Bath

Upgrades

Delve into a case study where strategic kitchen and bathroom upgrades played a pivotal role in enhancing a property's value. Explore the design choices, material selections, and market response that led to a successful resale.

Case Study 2: Curb Appeal Transformation

Explore a case study where a focus on enhancing curb appeal proved instrumental in attracting buyers. Analyze the landscaping, exterior renovations, and staging strategies that contributed to a quick and lucrative resale.

Case Study 3: Energy-Efficient and Smart Home

Renovations

Analyze a case study where incorporating energy-efficient and smart home features significantly increased the property's market appeal. Explore the investment in sustainable upgrades and the positive buyer response that followed.

From strategic planning to hands-on execution, each stage of the renovation process plays a crucial role in shaping a property's potential and marketability.

CHAPTER 11
Planning and Executing Renovations

Renovating a home is a critical component of real estate flipping, converting it from its current state to an attractive and marketable asset. Chapter 11 is a complete guide on planning and carrying out improvements properly. From strategic planning to careful execution, this chapter provides flippers with the information and tactics they need to maximize the value of their homes.

Assessing Property Potential

Understanding The Property's Condition

Before beginning repairs, it is critical to inspect the property's condition properly. Assess structural integrity, current features, and areas for improvement. Understanding the property's existing condition lays the groundwork for rehabilitation plans.

Identifying Renovation Opportunities.

Identify the areas of the property that have the most potential for improvement. Concentrate on areas that may dramatically increase the property's value and attractiveness, such as kitchens, bathrooms, and outside appeal. Prioritize improvements in line with market trends and consumer preferences.

Developing a Renovation Plan

Setting Clear Renovation Goals

Set specific remodeling goals based on the property's potential and intended market. Determine whether the goal is to increase resale value, target a certain buyer group, or develop a distinctive selling offer. Clear goals drive the refurbishment process and ensure it is consistent with the broader flipping strategy.

Developing a Comprehensive Budget

Create a precise remodeling budget that covers all costs, including materials, labor, permits, and contingencies. Consider market circumstances, local legislation, and possible cost drivers. A detailed budget helps to control spending and assures financial sustainability during the restoration project.

Selecting Renovation Projects

Prioritizing High-Impact Projects

Determine which remodeling projects have the best potential for impact and return on investment. Focus on modifications that improve the property's functioning, beauty, and marketability. Prioritize initiatives that resonate with target customers and are in line with market trends.

Balancing Cost and Value

Strike a balance between remodeling expenditures and the expected rise in property value. Evaluate the cost-effectiveness of each renovation project and select those with the best return on investment. Consider market demand, property comparisons, and the competitive situation.

Obtaining Necessary Permits and Approvals.

Understanding Regulatory Requirements

Familiarize yourself with the local building rules, zoning restrictions, and permit procedures for rehabilitation projects. Determine what permissions and approvals are required for the proposed modifications, including structural alterations, electrical work, plumbing upgrades, and additions.

Obtaining Permits and Approvals

Start the permit application procedure well before beginning improvements. Submit complete and correct documents to the appropriate authorities and follow up to guarantee timely approvals. Compliance with regulatory regulations reduces the risk of penalties, project delays, and legal complications.

Hiring Contractors and Managing Teams

Selecting Qualified Contractors

Carefully evaluate contractors and subcontractors based on their credentials, expertise, and reputation. Request references, analyze previous projects, and confirm licenses and insurance coverage. Choose contractors who exhibit professionalism, dependability, and a dedication to great work.

Establishing Clear Communication

Create open and transparent communication channels between contractors and project teams. Clearly explain project objectives, timeframes, and expectations from the start. Maintain constant communication during the refurbishment process to resolve any difficulties as they arise and to guarantee that the renovation plan is followed.

Implementing Sustainable and Energy-Efficient Practices

Embracing Sustainability

Include sustainable and energy-efficient strategies in

refurbishment projects to decrease environmental effects and running expenses. Consider energy-efficient appliances, LED lighting, low-flow fixtures, and environmentally friendly materials. Sustainable renovations attract environmentally concerned purchasers and help to ensure long-term sustainability.

Maximizing Energy Efficiency

Increase the property's energy efficiency via smart modifications and insulation enhancements. Consider things like insulation, windows, HVAC systems, and renewable energy sources. Maximizing energy efficiency increases the property's value, comfort, and appeal to potential purchasers.

Monitoring Progress and Quality Control

Regular Site Inspections

Conduct frequent site inspections to ensure progress, quality, and adherence to the remodeling plan. To avoid delays or cost overruns, address any deviations or difficulties as soon as they arise. Maintain detailed records of inspections, adjustments, and communications throughout the remodeling project.

Quality Assurance Checks

Implement quality assurance methods to guarantee that renovations meet the highest standards of craftsmanship and finish. Inspect finished work thoroughly and resolve any flaws or anomalies right away. Prioritize quality control to ensure that the completed product meets or exceeds the buyer's expectations.

Adding Value with Design and Finishes

Designing for Market Appeal

Interiors and finishes should be designed to appeal to

target purchasers while remaining current with design trends. Choose neutral color palettes, modern fixtures, and high-quality materials to improve the property's appearance and performance. Incorporate design elements that contribute to a unified and appealing ambiance.

Enhancing Curb Appeal

Improve the property's curb appeal via landscaping, exterior renovations, and attention to detail. To make a good first impression, invest in things like well-kept lawns, external lights, and fresh paint. Increasing curb appeal attracts purchasers and boosts the property's perceived worth.

Staging for Sales

Professional Staging Services

Engage expert staging services to highlight the property's potential and foster an emotional connection with purchasers. Set up important rooms and living areas to emphasize utility, flow, and lifestyle appeal. Use furniture, accessories, and design to create welcoming and aspirational spaces.

Virtual Staging and Digital Marketing

Use virtual staging and digital marketing tactics to reach a larger number of prospective buyers. Create high-quality images, virtual tours, and marketing materials that highlight the property's most prominent features and services. Use internet platforms and social media to increase interest and attract quality leads.

Case Studies: Renovation Success Stories

Investigate real-world case studies of successful remodeling projects that substantially aided the development of real estate flipping businesses. Analyze the actions, obstacles, and outcomes of expert flippers who completed restorations with outstanding results.

Case Study 1: Transformative Kitchen and Bath

Upgrades

Examine a case study in which judicious kitchen and bathroom modifications significantly increased a property's value and marketability. Analyze the design decisions, material selections, and consumer reactions that resulted in a successful resell.

Case Study 2: Comprehensive Exterior Renovations

Examine a case study in which thorough exterior upgrades increased the property's curb appeal and drew purchasers. Evaluate the landscaping, facade renovations, and staging methods that led to rapid and profitable sales.

Case Study 3: Energy-Efficient and Sustainable

Renovations

Analyze a case study in which energy-efficient and sustainable improvements increased the value of the home. Investigate the investment in eco-friendly features, consumer interest in sustainability, and the total effect on resale value.

From strategic planning to thorough execution, each stage of the remodeling process is critical to realizing the full potential of your property.

CHAPTER 11
Tips for Selling Your Home

Selling a house is the climax of the real estate flipping process, where the efforts made in purchase, remodeling, and marketing pay off. In Chapter 11, we look at key suggestions and methods for effectively selling a flipped home. From improving curb appeal to negotiating bids, this chapter gives practical advice for optimizing the selling process and maximizing returns on investment.

Enhancing Curb Appeal

First impressions count, and curb appeal is an important factor in enticing potential buyers. Invest in landscaping, grass care, and external improvements to create an inviting and visually pleasing façade. Ensure that the property's facade is in good condition, with new paint, clean windows, and appealing landscaping.

Pay attention to minor things that may boost curb appeal, such as new hardware, a clean doorway, and ornamental accents. Consider using outdoor lights to emphasize architectural details and create a cosy atmosphere. A neatly kept façade sets the tone for a pleasant viewing experience.

Designing the interior

Create a clean, neutral canvas that allows potential purchasers to imagine themselves living in it. To start fresh, declutter spaces, remove personal objects, and depersonalize design. Reduce distractions and create an open, welcoming environment that emphasizes the property's characteristics.

Invest in expert staging to highlight the property's potential and increase buyer interest. Arrange furniture and décor to improve traffic flow and showcase your main selling features. Create attractive and aspirational living environments by strategically placing lighting, decorations, and furnishings.

Pricing Strategy

Conduct thorough market research to establish the best listing price for your home. Determine a competitive pricing point by analyzing recent sales data, comparable properties, and current market trends. Price your home appropriately to attract buyers and maximize your return on investment.

Consider pricing tactics such as pricing slightly below market value to stimulate interest and many bids or prices at market value to get a more balanced result. Collaborate with your real estate agent to create a price plan that reflects your goals and market conditions.

Effective marketing

Invest in professional photography and videography to present your home in the best light. High-quality pictures capture the attention and interest of potential purchasers perusing internet listings. Capture the property's distinguishing traits and highlights to develop effective marketing materials.

Utilize a multi-channel marketing strategy to reach a large number of potential consumers. Use internet tools like listing websites, social media, and email marketing to market your home. To increase awareness, consider using offline marketing methods such as print advertising, open homes, and signage.

Open House and Showings

Plan and execute open houses efficiently to attract potential purchasers. Prepare the property for viewing, establish a friendly environment, and give guests with educational materials. Engage with potential buyers, answer their questions, and showcase the property's characteristics and advantages.

Schedule private showings for serious purchasers who have expressed interest in the property. Allow flexibility in scheduling to meet potential purchasers' preferences and availability. Give customers individualized tours and information to help them visualize themselves living in the location.

Handling Offers and Negotiations

Review and assess any offers received from possible purchasers. Consider the offer price, contingencies, financing terms, and closing timeframe. Collaborate with your real estate agent to evaluate each offer's merits and drawbacks and make educated selections.

Negotiate with purchasers to negotiate mutually advantageous terms and close the transaction. Maintain open communication and openness during the negotiating process. Negotiate effectively to ensure the greatest potential outcome for your interests while also meeting the buyer's demands.

Managing the Closing Process

Participate in the buyer's due diligence process by providing the relevant papers and access to the property. Address any issues or queries presented by the customer in a timely and open manner. Facilitate a seamless due diligence process to increase the buyer's trust and confidence.

Coordinate the closure with all parties involved, such as the buyer, seller, real estate agents, and closing agents. Ensure that all documentation is done correctly and on schedule. To ensure a smooth closing, coordinate logistics such as key and utility transfers.

Post-Sales Follow-Up

Follow up with the buyer after the transaction to guarantee their happiness and handle any post-sale problems. Provide tools and information to assist the buyer settle into their new home easily. Building strong connections with buyers generates goodwill and may result in referrals or future business.

Take time to reflect on the selling process and assess the lessons learnt. Determine areas of success and possibilities for improvement to guide future real estate flipping initiatives. Use input from buyers, brokers, and other stakeholders to improve your sales strategy.

CHAPTER 12
Determine The Listing Price

When it comes to purchasing a home, most potential purchasers will use the listing price as the number one factor to determine the homes that they look at.

Even though you and a realtor may determine the asking price, the client will determine the selling price. If the price is too excessive, most buyers won't give it a second thought - which is why you want to determine the listing price meticulously.

If you set the correct price, you'll observe a much quicker sale. Setting the correct listing price will also attract more potential purchasers to your property as well. You'll also observe an increase in response from realtors and receive more inquiries about the property. The listing price is essential - and it can ultimately determine whether or not you sell your property.

A property can be overvalued due to several reasons. Overpricing is something you want to avoid, as purchasers tend to steer clear of residences that have been overpriced. Normally, this occurs when a buyer requests a lot more than the home is worth or valued at.

Some buyers seek a lot more than the value of the property due to location. Although the location is essential, most potential buyers won't give the home a second glance if they believe the price is too high - and, more crucially, out of their price range.

When you place your home up for sale, most activity will happen within the first couple of weeks. If you put the correct price on your home, you'll observe immediate interest. There are always purchasers searching for homes in their price range, waiting for new homes to be listed or homes to be reduced in price.

Buyers who are waiting to purchase may only see your home completely if the price is reasonable.

To determine the listing price of your property, you should always have it appraised before you place it on the market. This way, you'll know the complete value of your residence. You can sell it for market value or go a little under, although you should never attempt to go way over the value. In doing so, you'll miss out on a number of potential customers. The home market is very competitive these days, which is why you want your home to generate as much interest as possible.

Realtors really have no control over the real estate market, only the plan behind marketing. Realtors don't determine the asking price - the seller does. You can consult a realtor for advice, although you are the judge of your listing price.

If you do things right and take each item step by step, you'll set the listing price in the correct area and have no problems selling your property.

CHAPTER 13
Legal and Regulatory Considerations

Navigating the legal and regulatory environment is critical for real estate flippers to assure compliance, limit risks, and safeguard their assets. In this Chapter, we dig into the difficult realm of legal and regulatory issues, arming flippers with the information and techniques required to overcome possible pitfalls and preserve their initiatives.

Zoning Laws and Land Use Regulations

Familiarize yourself with local zoning rules and land use restrictions controlling property development and rehabilitation. Understand zoning classifications, authorized property uses, setback requirements, and height limits. Ensure that your remodeling plans correspond with local standards to prevent expensive delays and fines.

Building Codes and Permits

Comply with building regulations and secure appropriate permissions for remodeling work. Understand the permit application procedure, needed documents, and inspection requirements. Failure to get permits or conform to construction rules may result in penalties, project delays, and legal responsibilities.

Contractual Agreements

Negotiate and sign purchase agreements that detail the terms and circumstances of property acquisition. Clarify critical elements such as purchase price, financing conditions, inspection periods, and closing dates. Work with legal specialists to examine and finish purchase agreements to safeguard your interests.

Contractor Agreements

Enter into formal contracts with contractors and subcontractors for remodeling projects. Specify project scope, dates, deliverables, and payment conditions in detail. Include procedures for dispute resolution, modification orders, and warranties to limit risks and maintain project responsibility.

Liability Insurance

Obtain enough liability insurance coverage to defend against any risks and liabilities involved with real estate flipping.

Consider coverage such as general liability insurance, property insurance, and errors and omissions insurance. Consult with insurance pros to determine your coverage requirements and get suitable policies.

Entity Structuring

Consider organizing your real estate flipping enterprises via legal structures such as limited liability companies (LLCs) or corporations to restrict personal responsibility and preserve your assets. Consult with legal and tax professionals to establish the most acceptable organizational structure based on your aims and circumstances.

Property Disclosures

Comply with statutory disclosure obligations by giving accurate and comprehensive information to potential purchasers. Disclose material problems, known concerns, and pertinent information regarding the property's condition, history, and any repairs or enhancements. Failure to disclose important information might lead to legal penalties and litigation.

Environmental Disclosures

Disclose any known environmental dangers or circumstances that may harm the property, such as lead-based paint, asbestos, or soil pollution. Understand federal, state, and local environmental disclosure obligations and assure compliance to prevent regulatory infractions and legal penalties.

Tax Implications

Capital Gains Tax

Understand the tax ramifications of real estate flipping, including capital gains tax on earnings from property transactions. Consult with tax specialists to maximize tax strategies, reduce tax payments, and take advantage of available deductions and credits.

Depreciation and Deductions

Explore options for depreciation and deductions connected to real estate investments, including depreciation of property renovations, mortgage interest deductions, and operational expenditures. Keep meticulous records of spending and engage with tax professionals to maximize tax advantages.

Mediation and Arbitration

Include provisions for alternative conflict resolution processes such as mediation or arbitration in commercial agreements to settle issues quickly and cost-effectively. Mediation and arbitration are non-adversarial ways of conflict settlement that assist in preventing prolonged litigation and protect corporate relationships.

Legal Remedies

Understand your legal rights and remedies in the case of contractual disputes, breaches, or other legal difficulties. Consult with legal specialists to discuss alternatives for enforcement, litigation, or settlement negotiations to defend your interests and obtain beneficial results.

Staying Informed

Stay updated on changes in laws, regulations, and market circumstances that may affect real estate flipping activity. Monitor legislative changes, regulatory updates, and industry trends to modify your strategy and procedures appropriately.

Continuing Education

Invest in continuing education and professional development to remain aware of legal and regulatory developments and best practices in real estate flipping. Attend seminars, workshops, and training programs given by recognized organizations and industry experts.

Ethical Standards

Adhere to ethical standards and professional behavior in all facets of real estate flipping. Maintain integrity, honesty, and openness in your relationships with customers, partners, contractors, and other stakeholders. Uphold ethical norms to develop trust and reputation in the sector.

Compliance Programs

Implement compliance processes and internal controls to guarantee conformity to legal and regulatory standards. Establish policies, processes, and training efforts to enhance compliance awareness and responsibility within your company.

CHAPTER 14

Risk Management in Real Estate Flipping

Risk management is a crucial aspect of real estate selling, as it involves sizable financial investments and possible market changes. This chapter will cover the various strategies and challenges involved with handling risks in real estate selling, offering a complete guide for real estate owners.

Understanding Risk in Real Estate Flipping

Market Risks

Market shifts, economic downturns, and changes in customer tastes can affect property prices and demand. Understand market patterns, local trends, and foreign factors that may affect real estate prices and sales activity. Diversify your assets and change your tactics to minimize exposure to market risks.

Financial Risks

Financial risks include problems such as cash flow shortages, unexpected costs, and funding challenges. Conduct thorough financial analysis and stress testing to measure the potential and success of real estate selling projects. Maintain appropriate cash and backup savings to cover unforeseen costs and reduce financial risks.

Identifying Potential Risks

Property-Specific Risks

Property-specific risks refer to factors such as position, state, and marketability of the land. Conduct thorough due diligence, property checks, and risk assessments to spot possible dangers, building issues, and other concerns. Evaluate the property's business prospects and risk profile before agreeing to a buy.

Legal and Regulatory Risks

Legal and regulatory dangers come from non-compliance with laws, rules, and contractual responsibilities. Stay informed about zoning laws, building rules, permit requirements, and environmental regulations that guide real estate operations. Consult with legal pros to ensure compliance and reduce legal risks throughout the switching process.

Strategies for Managing Risks in Real Estate Flipping

1. **Market study:** Conducting a full market study to understand the present and future trends in the chosen area. This includes assessing property demand, supply, and price factors.
2. **Financial Due Diligence:** Performing thorough financial due diligence to measure the investment's profitability, including the cost of purchase, remodeling, and possible selling value.
3. **Legal and Regulatory agreement:** Ensuring agreement with all legal and regulatory requirements, such as zoning laws, building rules, and permit regulations, to minimize legal risks.
4. **Insurance Coverage:** Securing appropriate insurance coverage, such as property insurance and liability insurance, to protect against unforeseen events, such as

natural disasters or accidents.

5. **Backup Planning:** Develop backup plans for unexpected delays, cost overruns, or market downturns to reduce the effect of unfavorable situations.
6. **Professional Partnerships:** Collaborating with experienced real estate agents, builders, and law experts to maximize their knowledge and minimize operating risks.
7. **Exit Strategies:** Formulating multiple exit strategies, such as selling, rental, or lease choices, to adapt to changing market conditions and reduce exposure to market instability.

Challenges in Real Estate Flipping Risk Management

1. **Value Complexity:** Valuing real estate properties and companies involves complex factors, such as asset value, debt assessment, and secret responsibilities, which can pose challenges in risk assessment.
2. **Hidden Liabilities:** Real estate companies may have hidden tax, debt, and environmental liabilities that are not represented in their net asset value (NAV), requiring careful evaluation to avoid unforeseen risks.
3. **Loss Exposure Identification:** Identifying and studying loss exposures is important for effective risk management, requiring thorough checks, due diligence, and a needs-based method to address clients' risk profiles.
4. **Default and Foreclosure Risks:** Real estate selling includes natural risks of default and foreclosure, requiring a clear understanding of mortgage requirements, lien responsibilities, and court processes to minimize these risks.

Effective risk management is integral to the success of real estate flipping, and investors must employ a comprehensive approach that encompasses market analysis, financial due diligence, legal compliance, and contingency planning to navigate the complexities and challenges of the real estate market.

CHAPTER 15

Scaling Your Real Estate Flipping Business

Scaling a real estate selling business includes carefully expanding operations, increasing project output, and improving efficiency to achieve growth and profits. In Chapter 15, we cover the essential factors and strategies for growing your real estate flipping business successfully. From leveraging technology to building a reliable team, this chapter provides practical insights to help you scale your business to new heights.

Setting Your Growth Strategy

Clarify your long-term goals and plans for growing your real estate flipping business. Determine key performance indicators (KPIs) such as project numbers, income targets, and market growth goals. Align your growth plan with your overall business goals to drive strategic decision-making and resource allocation.

Conduct market study and analysis to find rich chances for development and growth. Explore new markets, ignored areas, and untapped segments where your skills and resources can provide a competitive advantage. Evaluate market demand, competitors, and governmental factors to measure the possibility of growing your business in particular areas.

Leveraging Technology and Automation

Embrace technology solutions and digital tools to simplify processes, improve efficiency, and grow your real estate flipping businesses. Explore project management software, virtual teamwork tools, and property management platforms to simplify routine chores, improve communication, and organize project data. Leverage data analytics and business intelligence tools to gain insights into market trends, project success, and funding possibilities.

Standardize processes, methods, and systems to improve speed and clarity across tasks. Automate regular jobs such as property analysis, project schedules, and financial reports to reduce human effort and limit mistakes. Implement regular forms, plans, and processes to simplify operations and keep quality standards as you grow your business.

Building a Reliable Team

Invest in hiring, teaching, and building a skilled team of professionals to support your real estate selling business. Hire experienced professionals such as project managers, builders, architects, and real estate salespeople with knowledge in their various areas. Provide ongoing training, mentoring, and professional development chances to strengthen your team and create a culture of constant learning and growth.

Delegate duties and encourage team members to take control of their jobs and add to the success of the business. Establish clear jobs, responsibilities, and standards to promote responsibility and cooperation. Encourage open conversation, feedback, and idea sharing to utilize the combined knowledge and innovation of your team.

Strategic Partnerships and Collaborations

Collaborate with industry partners, sellers, and service providers to grow your network and access important resources and knowledge. Build smart relationships with real estate agents, lenders, builders, and suppliers who share your vision and beliefs. Leverage relationships to access off-market deals, secure favorable financing terms, and ease project execution.

Explore possibilities for joint partnerships and syndications to pool resources, share risks, and grow your real estate selling business. Partner with funders, developers, and other partners to tackle bigger projects, spread investments, and build on joint strengths. Establish clear deals, control frameworks, and communication routes to ensure openness and matching of interests among parties.

Financial Planning and Capital Allocation

Develop a thorough financial plan to support your business growth and development efforts. Evaluate different financial choices such as standard bank loans, private equity, crowdfunding, and joint partnerships. Assess the cost of cash, terms, and risks involved with each financing choice to determine the most suitable method for funding your growing efforts.

Optimize capital allocation and resource allocation to maximize profits and minimize risks as you grow your real estate flipping business. Allocate funds carefully across projects, markets, and financial options to spread risk and improve profits. Monitor project success, cash flow, and return on investment (ROI) to make data-driven choices and change resource sharing as required.

Monitoring and Evaluation

Establish and watch key performance indicators (KPIs) to track progress, measure success, and find areas for change as you grow your real estate selling business. Monitor KPIs such as project revenue, ROI, project timelines, and customer happiness to assess business success and the usefulness of growing strategies. Utilize data analytics and reporting tools to gain insights into trends, patterns, and chances for improvement.

Foster a mindset of ongoing change and innovation within

your company to drive lasting growth and success. Encourage feedback, experimenting, and learning from both wins and mistakes. Adapt and improve your growth strategies based on market feedback, industry trends, and changing customer wants to stay agile and flexible in a dynamic business environment.

CHAPTER 16

Common Risks Faced by Property Flippers

Real estate flipping provides profitable prospects for investors, but it also comes with its fair share of pitfalls. Here we cover the main hazards encountered by property flippers and ways for successfully managing and minimizing these risks. By knowing and proactively addressing possible problems, flippers may boost their chances of success and preserve their assets in the competitive real estate market.

Market Risks

Fluctuations in the economy, such as recessions or economic downturns, may affect property prices and demand for real estate. Property flippers may encounter difficulty in selling homes or may see a reduction in property prices during moments of economic instability. Mitigation techniques include diversifying assets, preserving liquidity buffers, and doing rigorous market research to spot developing trends.

Market saturation happens when there is an overstock of properties or an invasion of flippers vying for the same market sector. This may lead to more competition, downward pressure on prices, and longer holding periods for properties. Flippers should undertake market research to uncover underdeveloped niches or new markets and customize their services to stand out in a crowded market.

Financial Risks

Cash flow constraints may develop when costs exceed income, resulting in liquidity issues and significant project delays. Flippers should carefully estimate and predict project spending, monitor cash flow regularly, and preserve contingency reserves to handle unforeseen costs. Additionally, getting finance or lines of credit might give a financial safety net during difficult moments.

Overleveraging happens when flippers take on excessive debt or leverage to fund property purchases and renovations. High amounts of debt raise financial risk and sensitivity to interest rate swings or market downturns. Flippers should use prudence while leveraging and maintaining a cautious debt-to-equity ratio to minimize overexposure to financial risk.

Property-Specific Risks

Properties with structural difficulties or costly repairs may represent considerable dangers to flippers. Unexpected structural difficulties may cause cost overruns, project delays, and significant safety risks. Flippers should do comprehensive property inspections and assessments to uncover structural concerns early and budget appropriately for repairs or improvements.

Properties with environmental dangers such as lead-based paint, asbestos, or mold offer health and liability risks to flippers. Failure to manage environmental dangers may result in regulatory infractions, legal penalties, and diminished property values. Flippers should do environmental evaluations and cleanup as required to guarantee compliance with standards and preserve inhabitants' health.

Legal and Regulatory Risks

Non-compliance with zoning rules, construction codes, licenses, or contractual commitments may result in fines, penalties, and legal challenges. Flippers should be aware of local legislation, secure relevant permissions, and maintain compliance with all legal requirements throughout the flipping process. Consulting with legal specialists and completing due diligence may assist in reducing legal issues.

Contractual disagreements with contractors, suppliers, or purchasers may interrupt project timetables and result in financial losses. Flippers should sign into formal contracts with specific terms and conditions, including dispute resolution systems. Maintaining open communication, recording agreements, and resolving conflicts peacefully may help limit legal and financial concerns.

Marketability Risks

Improvement happens when flippers commit excessive money to repairs or improvements that do not fit with market demand or property prices. Over-improved homes may fail to attract purchasers or attain anticipated resale prices, resulting in decreased returns on investment. Flippers should perform market research and concentrate on cost-effective upgrades that optimize property value and appeal to potential purchasers.

Marketing issues such as inefficient advertising, poor staging, or restricted visibility may hinder property sales and profitability. Flippers should build thorough marketing strategies, harness online and offline media, and present property attributes efficiently to attract possible purchasers. Investing in excellent photography, staging services, and focused marketing efforts may boost property marketability and speed up sales.

External Risks

Natural catastrophes such as hurricanes, floods, or wildfires may cause property damage and impede real estate flipping efforts. Flippers should examine property location and exposure to natural disasters, seek insurance coverage for property damage, and undertake disaster preparation steps to limit risk. Collaborating with local authorities and emergency services may boost resilience and response skills during crises.

External variables such as changes in interest rates, tax laws, or government restrictions may affect property prices and market dynamics. Flippers should be educated about macroeconomic trends, legislative developments, and regulatory changes that may affect real estate markets. Adopting a proactive approach to risk management and modifying methods in reaction to external events may help limit risks and capitalize on opportunities.

CHAPTER 17
Learning from Case Studies

Case studies provide unique insights into real-world circumstances, teaching flippers practical lessons, techniques, and best practices for success in the real estate flipping business. In this Chapter, we will look at a number of case studies that demonstrate the various experiences, obstacles, and results faced by property flips. By reviewing these case studies, flippers may learn important lessons, uncover common dangers, and apply tried-and-true tactics to their real estate flipping endeavors.

Case Study 1: Strategic Renovation Maximizes Profitability.

Overview: In this case study, a house flipper achieved maximum profit via smart refurbishment and market placement.
Challenges: The property previously had substantial visual and functional flaws, necessitating considerable repairs to increase market value.

Strategies:

- Conducted market research to understand customer preferences and trends.
- It created a strategic refurbishment strategy centered on high-impact enhancements that were consistent with target buyer demographics and preferences.
- Cost-effective modifications were implemented to

improve the property's beauty, usefulness, and marketability.
- We used expert staging and photography to highlight home qualities and attract prospective buyers.

Outcomes:
- Significantly increased home value and market attractiveness.
- Strong buyer interest resulted in numerous competing bids.
- The flipper made significant gains since the home sold for more than the asking amount.

Lessons learned:
- Strategic refurbishment and market positioning are critical drivers of profit in real estate flipping.
- Understanding consumer preferences and market trends is critical for targeting upgrades successfully.
- Investing in expert staging and marketing may greatly improve home marketability and sales results.

Case Study 2: overcoming adversity in a challenging market.

Overview: This case study shows how a property flipper overcame difficulties and found success in a difficult market climate.

Challenge: The flipper faced unforeseen delays, cost overruns, and market downturns throughout the restoration and selling process.

Strategies:
- For proactive and collaborative problem-solving include maintaining open communication with contractors, suppliers, and stakeholders.
- Implemented contingency planning and risk mitigation strategies to successfully manage project delays and cost overruns.
- Marketing strategy and pricing approaches were adapted to reflect changing market circumstances and

    customer preferences.
- We utilized innovative finance alternatives and negotiating tactics to get favorable terms and optimize profits.

Outcome:
- Successfully finished the project despite unexpected hurdles and market uncertainty.
- Effective risk management and adaptability helped to reduce financial losses and maintain project profitability.
- Positioned the property competitively in the market and completed the sale within a reasonable timeline.

Lessons Learned:
- Success in real estate flipping requires flexibility, perseverance, and adaptation to overcome problems.
- Effective project uncertainty management requires proactive communication, contingency planning, and risk reduction methods.
- In difficult market conditions, flippers might benefit from creative finance and negotiating abilities to get advantageous terms and overcome financial barriers.

Case Study 3: Avoiding Pitfalls with Diligent Due Diligence

Overview: This case study emphasizes the significance of doing thorough due diligence to mitigate risks and prevent hazards in real estate flipping ventures.

Challenges: Inadequate due research resulted in unanticipated structural difficulties and regulatory breaches for the flipper.

Strategies:
- Conducted thorough property inspections and evaluations to detect risks, faults, and regulatory concerns.
- Professional professionals such as inspectors, engineers,

and legal consultants were hired to assess the property's condition and compliance.

- We have obtained the essential licenses and permissions to meet regulatory requirements and assure compliance with zoning regulations and building standards.
- She negotiated with sellers, contractors, and other stakeholders to successfully resolve identified concerns and risks.

Outcome:

- Successfully addressed structural concerns and regulatory infractions via aggressive involvement and negotiation.
- By dealing with compliance concerns in a timely and responsible manner, we avoided expensive legal fights, fines, and penalties.
- Completed the project with minimal interruptions and successfully sold within the estimated dates and budget.

Lessons Learned:

- Real estate flipping ventures need thorough due diligence to identify and handle any risks and liabilities.
- Engaging experienced specialists and performing comprehensive inspections may assist in finding hidden concerns and efficiently managing hazards.
- Proactive involvement and negotiation help avoid expensive legal conflicts and regulatory infractions, maintaining project profitability and success.

CHAPTER 18

The Future of Real Estate Flipping

The real estate flipping industry has evolved considerably over the years, driven by technological advancements, demographic shifts, and altering market dynamics. In Chapter 18, we explore emerging trends, innovative technologies, and future opportunities influencing the landscape of real estate flipping. By anticipating future developments and adapting strategies accordingly, traders can position themselves for success in an evolving market.

Technological Innovations

Virtual Reality (VR) and Augmented Reality (AR)

VR and AR technologies are revolutionizing the real estate industry by offering immersive virtual experiences for property viewing and visualization. Flippers can leverage VR and AR tools to demonstrate properties, stage virtual renovations, and engage purchasers remotely, augmenting marketing effectiveness and accelerating sales cycles.

Artificial Intelligence (AI) and Machine Learning

AI and machine learning algorithms can analyze enormous quantities of data to identify market trends, predict property values, and optimize investment decisions. Flippers can use AI-driven analytics platforms to assess property investment opportunities, evaluate renovation strategies, and identify potential risks, facilitating data-driven decision-making and superior investment outcomes.

Sustainable and Green Flipping

Energy-Efficient Renovations

Growing awareness of environmental sustainability and energy efficiency is propelling demand for green renovations in real estate flipping. Flippers can integrate energy-efficient features such as solar panels, smart thermostats, and energy-efficient appliances to entice eco-conscious purchasers and enhance property value while reducing environmental impact.

Sustainable Materials and Practices

The use of sustainable building materials and construction practices is becoming increasingly prevalent in real estate conversion initiatives. Flippers can prioritize environmentally responsible materials such as reclaimed wood, recycled materials, and low-VOC coatings to minimize carbon footprint and promote sustainability in property renovations.

Demographic Trends

Aging Population

The aging population presents new opportunities for real estate developers to accommodate the requirements of senior individuals seeking age-friendly housing options. Flippers can adapt properties to integrate universal design features such as grasp bars, wheelchair ramps, and accessible restrooms to appeal to seniors and retirees looking for comfortable and safe living environments.

Millennial Homebuyers

Millennials represent a significant demographic segment generating demand for affordable, move-in-ready residences in urban and suburban markets. Flippers can target millennial purchasers by renovating properties to satisfy their preferences for modern amenities, open floor plans, and smart home technology, facilitating quicker sales and maximizing returns on investment.

Regulatory and Policy Changes

Zoning Reforms

Zoning reforms and regulatory changes aimed at increasing housing affordability and density may present opportunities for real estate developers to develop infill properties or repurpose underutilized spaces.

Flippers can capitalize on relaxed zoning restrictions and streamlined permitting processes to undertake innovative projects and satisfy evolving market demand.

Rent Control and Tenant Protection

Rising concerns about housing affordability and tenant rights may lead to increased rent control measures and tenant protections in certain markets. Flippers should remain informed about regulatory changes and consider the potential impact on property values, rental yields, and investment feasibility when evaluating real estate converting opportunities in rent-controlled jurisdictions.

Shifts in Consumer Preferences

Remote Work and Home Office Spaces

The rise of remote work and flexible work arrangements is fueling demand for home office spaces and dedicated remote work amenities in residential properties. Flippers can capitalize on this trend by implementing functional home office designs, high-speed internet connectivity, and ergonomic workstations to attract remote workers and telecommuters.

Wellness and Lifestyle Amenities

Consumers are increasingly prioritizing wellness and lifestyle amenities in their residential properties, such as outdoor spaces, fitness facilities, and community gardens.

Flippers can differentiate their properties by integrating wellness features and amenities that promote health, relaxation, and community engagement, appealing to discerning purchasers desiring a holistic living experience.

CONCLUSION:
Your Path to Successful Real Estate Flipping

Congratulations on finishing your adventure in real estate flipping! In this thorough book, we've covered every step of the real estate flipping process, from purchase to rehab to sale. With the information and tactics provided in this book, you are well-prepared to start your profitable real estate flipping business.

Take time to reflect on your adventure. You've learned how to find profitable investment prospects, perform in-depth property analyses, and manage the complexity of financing and purchase. You have developed your talents in strategic renovation planning, high-impact enhancements, and effective renovation team management. You've perfected the art of promoting and selling real estate, attracting buyers, negotiating offers, and completing agreements with confidence.

Celebrate your accomplishments and milestones along the road. Whether it's completing your first flip, obtaining a higher-than-expected resale value, or overcoming obstacles and disappointments, each achievement demonstrates your commitment and tenacity. Accept the lessons learned from both achievements and mistakes, as they will provide useful insights for future initiatives.

When planning future real estate flipping initiatives, keep in mind that the path is continuing. The real estate industry is dynamic and ever-changing, bringing new possibilities and problems with every project. Stay up to date on market trends, new technology, and industry best practices to stay competitive and adaptive in today's fast-paced real estate market.

Continue to educate yourself and broaden your expertise in all elements of real estate flipping. Learn about advanced subjects, including commercial real estate, multi-unit buildings, and real estate development, to diversify your portfolio and extend your investing prospects. Network with industry leaders, attend seminars and conferences and seek mentoring from experienced flippers to speed up your learning and advancement.

As you continue your real estate flipping adventure, consider passing on your expertise and experiences to others. Mentor budding flippers, contribute to online forums and groups, and attend local real estate events to encourage and empower other investors. Giving back to the real estate community not only improves people's lives but also contributes to the industry's overall success.

As you begin your journey to successful real estate flipping, remember that tenacity, resilience, and a desire to learn are the keys to long-term success. Accept setbacks as chances for progress, be optimistic, and always maintain sight of your objectives. With dedication, hard effort, and a commitment to perfection, you may accomplish your goals and leave a legacy of success in the world of real estate flipping.

ABOUT THE AUTHOR

Katherine R. Walters

 Katherine R. Walters has been engaged in various real estate deals over the previous 21 years. She is actively investing in real estate around the nation, from flipping to wholesaling to rents, commercials, and more! Her blueprint book is packed with ideas, methods, formulae, and secrets that she employs in her company in the present market. they are not old ideals or misleading promises; they are concrete tasks you can accomplish now! With a focus on safe investment for greater returns, she has utilized her real estate assessment experience as the background for giving information that may alter your life!

In between his real estate ventures, Katherine and his family enjoy the rewards of their work by traversing the globe. Real estate investment might be the key to improving your future.

Besides writing, Katherine is still actively trading in several markets. She is the owner of a real estate agency in Seattle, WA (Shipwright Realty), where She teaches her Realtors numerous financial tactics and still travels the globe with her family.

www.ingramcontent.com/pod-product-compliance
Lightning Source LLC
Chambersburg PA
CBHW070026260726
48658CB00002B/511